D0744145

Football's All-Time Greats

LINEBACKERS

JOSH LEVENTHAL

BLACK
RABBIT
BOOKS

Bolt is published by Black Rabbit Books
P.O. Box 3263, Mankato, Minnesota, 56002.
www.blackrabbitbooks.com
Copyright © 2017 Black Rabbit Books

Design and Production by Michael Sellner
Photo Research by Rhonda Milbrett

Library of Congress Control Number: 2015954844

HC ISBN: 978-1-68072-040-2   PB ISBN: 978-1-68072-298-7

Printed in the United States at CG Book Printers,
North Mankato, Minnesota, 56003. PO #1796 4/16

Web addresses included in this book were working and appropriate
at the time of publication. The publisher is not responsible for broken
or changed links.

Image Credits
AP Images: ASSOCIATED PRESS, 9,
10, 11, 13 (top); 20 (middle); Greg Trott,
6-7 (middle); NFL, 16, 20 (left & right); Paul Spi-
nelli, 18; Tom DiPace, 21 (left); Vernon J. Biever, 12;
Winslow Townson, 19; Corbis: David Richard/AP, Cover;
Cliff Welch/Icon Sportswire, 7; John Pyle/ZUMA Press, 6;
Getty: George Gojkovich, 15; Newscom: Evan Pike/Cal Sport
Media, 21 (right); GEORGE BRIDGES/KRT, 24; HARRY WALK-
ER/KRT, 21 (middle); Jim Dedmon/Icon Sportswire CDA, 27;
John Pyle/Cal Sport Media, 26; Rob Tringali SportsChrome, 1,
Back Cover; St Petersburg Times/ZUMAPRESS, 23; TROY WAY-
RYNEN/UPI, 4-5; WD/Icon SMI 480/WD/Icon SMI, 29 (top);
Shutterstock: EKS, 3, 6-7 (background), 20-21 (background);
enterlinedesign, 28-29 (bottom); Orgus88, 13 (bottom);
Svyatoslav Aleksandrov, 31; VitaminCo, 32
Every effort has been made to contact copyright
holders for material reproduced in this book.
Any omissions will be rectified in subse-
quent printings if notice is given
to the publisher.

Contents

CHAPTER 1

Leading

the Defense

The linebacker stands ready on the field. The other team's quarterback yells, "hike!" He prepares to throw the ball. But the linebacker sees a hole in the line of **defenders**. Before the quarterback can throw, the linebacker tackles him. It's a

sack!

LINEBACKER'S TACKLE

move feet in **small, quick steps**

squat low

swing arms .... around the other player

Step 1

Step 2

6

push shoulder ···· into ····→ the other player

keep pushing until the other player is down

Step 3

CHAPTER 2

Linebackers

from 1920 to 1965

Linebackers are a big part of a team's defense. They help stop other teams' **running backs**. They also help stop other teams' passes.

Long ago, teams used two linebackers for each play. In the 1950s, teams added a third linebacker. This new position made defenses even stronger.

9

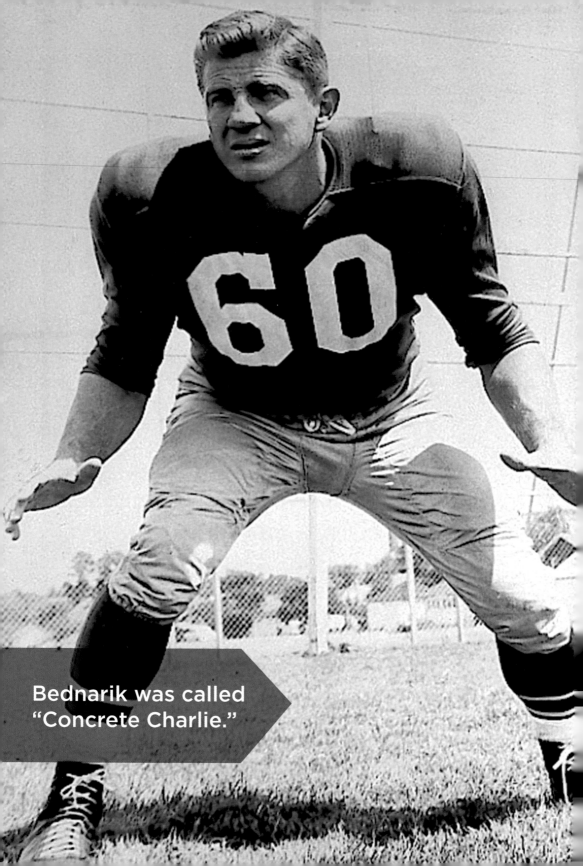

Bednarik was called "Concrete Charlie."

Chuck Bednarik and
Bill George · · · · · · · · · · · ·

Chuck Bednarik was known for his powerful tackles. He played linebacker for the Eagles. He also played on the team's **offense**.

Bill George changed linebackers' job. He was the first linebacker to try to stop passes. He had 18 **career interceptions**.

Ray Nitschke

Ray Nitschke played with the Packers. He helped them win five championships. In his career, he recovered 20 **fumbles**.

Sam Huff

Sam Huff was a fierce hitter. And he was fast. Huff played for the Giants and the Redskins. He had 30 interceptions in his career.

Players in the Hall of Fame by Position

33 Quarterbacks
25 Receivers
46 Running Backs
8 Tight Ends
4 Kickers/Punters
27 Linebackers

(through 2016)

CHAPTER 3

Linebackers

from 1966 to 1999

The late 1960s through the 1990s were a time of change. Linebackers became more aggressive. They went after **opponents**. They didn't wait for opponents to get to them.

Jack Lambert

Dick Butkus

Dick Butkus and Jack Lambert

Dick Butkus was one of the most feared players in the **NFL**. He would rip the ball from other players' hands. He recovered 27 fumbled balls in his career.

Jack Lambert was a linebacker for the Steelers. Some people call him the toughest tackler of all time. He made 1,479 tackles in his career. He also had more than 20 sacks.

Lawrence Taylor

Many think Lawrence Taylor is the greatest linebacker ever. He was fast and tough. He even played when he was hurt. Taylor never gave up.

Most Career Sacks by Linebackers
from 1982 to 2015

1. Kevin Greene	**160.0**
2. DeMarcus Ware	134.5
3. Lawrence Taylor	**132.5**
4. Rickey Jackson	**128.0**
5. Derrick Thomas	126.5

Sacks were not counted before 1982.

Junior Seau

Junior Seau played 20 seasons in the
NFL. His quick, powerful style made
him a great linebacker. He had
56.5 career sacks and
18 interceptions.

SIZE THEM UP

HEIGHT (inches)

Player	Height	Weight
Chuck Bednarik	75" (191 cm)	233 (106 kg)
Bill George	74" (188 cm)	237 (108 kg)
Sam Huff	73" (185 cm)	230 (104 kg)
Ray Nitschke	75" (191 cm)	235 (107 kg)
Dick Butkus	75" (191 cm)	245 (111 kg)
Jack Lambert	76" (193 cm)	220 (100 kg)

76"
75"
74"
73"
72"
71"
70"
69"

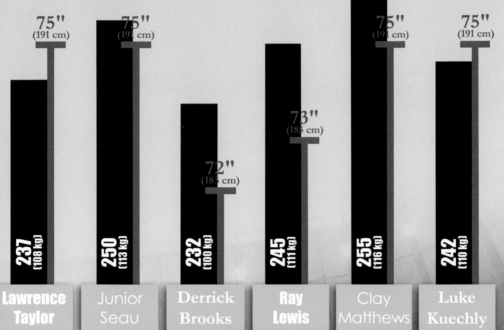

WEIGHT
(pounds)

255
250
245
240
235
230
225
220
215
210
205
200
195
190
185

75"
(191 cm)

75"
(191 cm)

75"
(191 cm)

75"
(191 cm)

73"
(185 cm)

72"
(185 cm)

237
(108 kg)

250
(113 kg)

232
(100 kg)

245
(111 kg)

255
(116 kg)

242
(110 kg)

| Lawrence Taylor | Junior Seau | Derrick Brooks | Ray Lewis | Clay Matthews | Luke Kuechly |

from 2000 to Today

Linebackers today are faster and stronger than ever. Some are good at stopping running backs. Others make lots of interceptions. The best linebackers do both.

Derrick Brooks

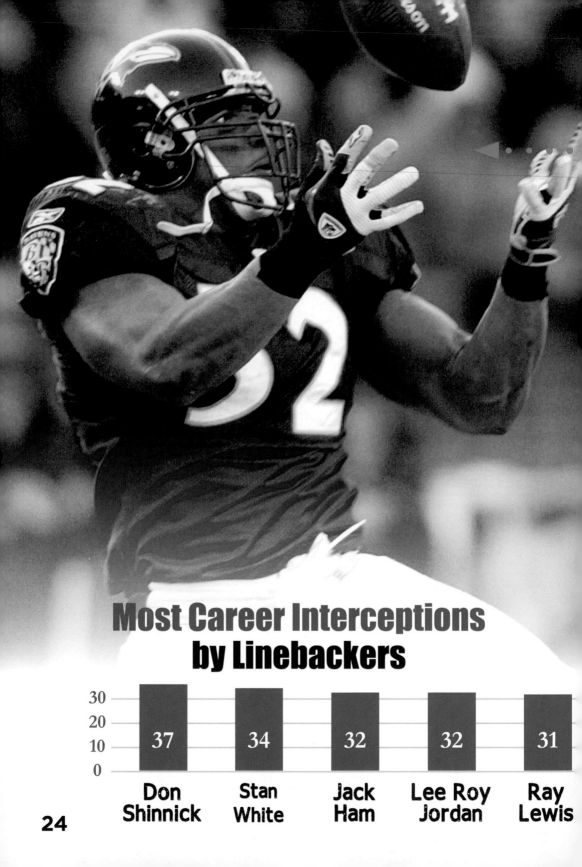

Most Career Interceptions by Linebackers

37	**34**	**32**	**32**	**31**
Don Shinnick	Stan White	Jack Ham	Lee Roy Jordan	Ray Lewis

Derrick Brooks and Ray Lewis

Derrick Brooks played for 14 years. He never missed a game. Brooks had a record five interceptions in 2002. He returned three of them for touchdowns.

Ray Lewis played with the Ravens. He was a leader and tough player. He was in the Pro Bowl 13 times. No other linebacker has gone that many times.

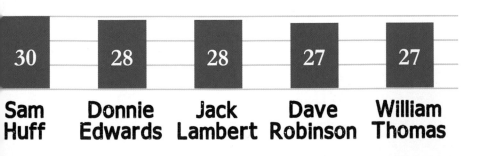

| 30 | 28 | 28 | 27 | 27 |
| Sam Huff | Donnie Edwards | Jack Lambert | Dave Robinson | William Thomas |

Clay Matthews

Clay Matthews is a linebacker for the Packers. He went to the Pro Bowl in five of his first six seasons. Matthews' father, grandfather, and brother all played in the NFL too.

Luke Kuechly

Luke Kuechly plays linebacker for the Panthers. He was Rookie of the Year in 2012. Fans are excited to see what records he breaks.

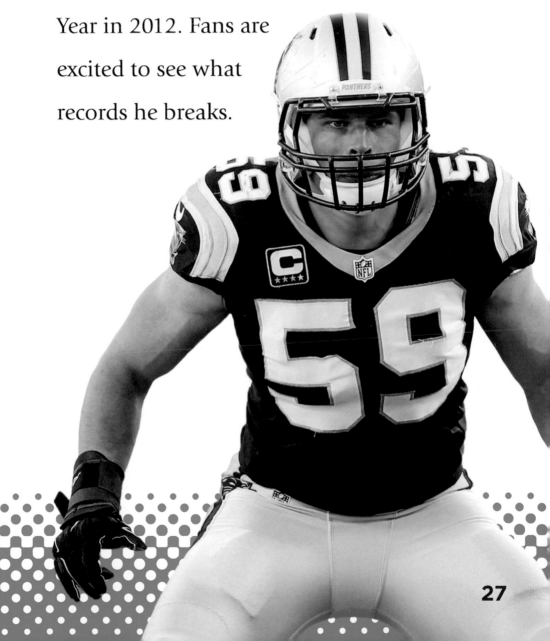

Tackling the Win

Teams need strong linebackers. These tough athletes scare quarterbacks. And they help stop other teams from scoring. They tackle for the win.

1925

October 1929
Great Depression begins

September 1939
World War II begins

July 1969
first moon landing

1950s
Teams add a third linebacker.

1952–1966
Bill George becomes first linebacker to try to stop passes.

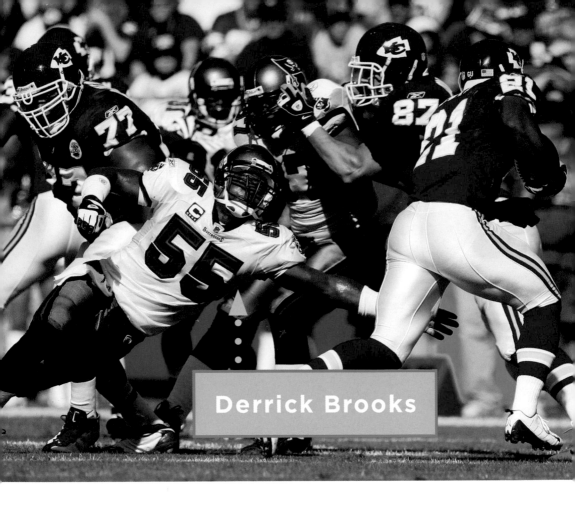

Derrick Brooks

September 2001
terrorist attack on World
Trade Center and Pentagon

1968
Don Shinnick
sets a record
with 37 career
interceptions.

1999
Kevin Greene
sets a record
with 160
career sacks.

2011
Ray Lewis sets
record for
most Pro Bowls
for a linebacker.

2015

GLOSSARY

career (kuh-REER)—a period of time spent in a job

defender (de-FEN-dur)—a player who is assigned to a defensive position

fumble (FUM-buhl)—a ball that is loose because a player failed to hold on to it

interception (in-tur-SEP-shun)—a catch made by a player from the opposing team

NFL—short for National Football League

offense (AW-fens)—the group of players in control of the ball trying to score points

opponent (uh-POH-nunt)—a person, team, or group that is competing against another

running back (RUN-ing BAK)—a player who carries the football on running plays

sack (SAK)—a tackle of the quarterback before he passes, hands off, or crosses the line of scrimmage

BOOKS

Challen, Paul. *What Does a Linebacker Do?* Football Smarts. New York: PowerKids Press, 2015.

Rausch, David. *National Football League.* Major League Sports. Minneapolis: Bellwether Media, Inc., 2015.

Scheff, Matt. *Superstars of the New York Giants.* Pro Sports Superstars. Mankato, MN: Amicus High Interest, 2014.

WEBSITES

Football: Linebacker
www.ducksters.com/sports/football/linebacker.php

Pro Football Hall of Fame
www.profootballhof.com